A SIX WEEK DEVOTIONAL
AND GROUP STUDY GUIDE

DR. NATE RUCH

THIS MATTERS

Small Group Study Guide
Edition 1.1
Copyright © 2019 Emmanuel

Requests for information should be addressed to:
Emmanuel
7777 University Ave. NE
Spring Lake Park, MN 55432

ISBN-9781089009955

TABLE OF CONTENTS

CONTENTS

ACKNOWLEDGMENTS

We have an amazing team at Emmanuel that has taken this message and developed it into a dynamic resource. Thank you to our Emmanuel pastors and staff for all of the inspiring devotions which were written by Ben Breit, Sara Breit, Dr. Lori Dykstra, Nathan Grams, Phil Johnson, Sydney Johnson, Emily Keymon, Paul Kelly, James Martinez, Andrew Mason, Jimmy Papia, Jodi Ruch, Jeff Ruch, Tim Sanders, Mark Alan Schoolmeesters, Jen Smith, Tim Smith, Jonathan Thomas, Bryan Talso, JonCarlos Velez and Michele Velez. Thank you to Julia Cummings for coordinating communication and content on this project. Thank you to Laura Wegener for her editing skills. Thank you to Andrew Baccam and Bri Cordle for their excellence on the overall design and format of this study guide. Thank you to Mark Alan Schoolmeester, JonCarlos Velez, Mark Nimmo and our Emmanuel Live team for their anointed efforts on the incredible worship videos that work with this study guide. Thank you to Sara Wescott and our Emmanuel Creative team for their filming and editing on all of the video resources. This would not have been possible without all of you!

WHAT MATTERS IN LIFE?

We live in day where we feel busier in our lives than ever and yet, we don't necessarily feel more fulfilled.

With so many demands and so much information coming at us, it can be difficult to know WHAT MATTERS. So what does matter? THIS MATTERS!

In this six-week group experience you can discover how to live with purpose and it starts with discovering what matters the most.

We're going to look at what's absolutely essential in core areas of our life. We're going to look at the following topics...

1. You Matter
2. Room for This
3. Family Matters
4. This is Us
5. The Office (Matters)
6. The Neighborhood Matters

We want to encourage you not to go on this journey alone. Make an effort to gather with a few friends and/or family members around these life impacting sessions and grow together.

HOW TO GET THE MOST OUT OF THIS STUDY GUIDE:

Here is a brief explanation of the features of this study guide.

- **Group curriculum** that allows you to follow along for each group discussion. The curriculum works alongside This Matters videos. The video series is 6 group sessions that each include a teaching video to launch into a group discussion as well as worship video content to use for the closing prayer time.
- **Scripture Memory** verses for each week.
- **Different individual and group activities** to further apply the principles and truths presented each week.
- **Five daily devotions** for each week for reading and inspiration. Each devotional includes a short prayer to launch your prayer time for the day.
- **"Notes"** are designated spaces for daily reflection and journal entries.
- **Resources** are in the back of the book for hosting your own This Matters Group

SESSION 1:
YOU MATTER

SCRIPTURE MEMORY

"You made all the delicate, inner parts of my body and knit me together in my mother's womb. Thank you for making me so wonderfully complex! Your workmanship is marvelous—how well I know it." – *Psalm 139:13-14 NLT*

WELCOME

During this first session, focus for the first ten minutes on getting to know each other. Serving light snacks and playing some upbeat Christian music in the background will help set the tone.

CHECKING IN

If this is the first meeting for this group, spend some time introducing yourselves. This also applies if a few new people have been added to an established group.

ASK: In about thirty seconds, introduce yourself and tell us why you are a part of this group.

REVIEW: On page 137-138 of this study guide, you will find the Small Group Guidelines. Take a few minutes and quickly look them over together.

ASK: Share a time when someone made you feel special.

PLAY SESSION 1A OF THIS MATTERS VIDEO SERIES AND WRITE DOWN ANYTHING THAT STANDS OUT TO YOU FROM THE TEACHING.

GROUP DISCUSSION QUESTIONS

#1 READ ALOUD: In our world today, there are many voices telling us that we don't matter. Or we don't matter as much as someone else. This results in feelings of insignificance, as explained in the video.

> **ASK:** Why is it so crucial to hear how God views us in the midst of so many negative voices?

> **READ ALOUD:** Pastor Nate spoke about some of the characteristics of the Insignificant Mentality. How have you seen these play out? As a reminder, the characteristics include:
> - Limited Prayer Life
> - Motivation-less Living
> - Shrinking back from Service
> - Procrastination
> - Focus on Vocation, rather than Relating
> - Missed Opportunities to Love People

#2 ASK SOMEONE READ ALOUD: Psalm 139:13-18 NLT

> **ASK:** What does this passage say about how God sees us?

> **ASK:** What stands out to you as being different from how we normally view ourselves?

> **ASK:** If this message was something we embraced on a daily basis, how might things change?

#3 READ OUT LOUD: Pastor Nate spoke about four things that God's vision of us brings. They include passion, motivation, direction, and purpose.

> **ASK:** Is there one of these you are lacking and/or you need the most right now in your life? Explain.

WORSHIP AND PRAYER TIME

PRAYER REQUESTS:
Ask for everyone's prayer requests. Encourage everyone to share their requests briefly so you can spend more time praying for your requests than talking about them. Be sure to record them on the Small Group Prayer and Praise Report on pages 140-141 of this study guide. Commit to pray for each other's requests every day of the week. Once all the requests are gathered, move into a group worship time.

GROUP WORSHIP & PRAYER TIME:

Before you pray for each other, invite the presence of the Lord into your time by playing the worship video for this week (Session 1B). As the worship time concludes, flow into your time of prayer by praying over the prayer requests. Encourage the group to participate by praying for one of the prayer requests that were listed.

PRAYER NOTE:
If praying in a group is new or uncomfortable for you, we encourage you to start by praying single-sentence prayers. Don't worry about how fancy you sound. God isn't looking for eloquence. He just wants honesty. Talk to God like you talk to a friend. Give everyone a chance to pray, but don't insist on it. Over time, you will all feel much more comfortable praying together.

DISMISSAL:
• Talk about the next group meeting.
• Encourage each other to continue to pray for each other throughout the week.
• Encourage group members to invite anyone they think will benefit from being in the group to the next meeting.
• Share basic contact information such as phone numbers and email addresses for your group members. The Small Group Roster on page 139 of this study guide is a good place to record this information.

JOURNALING ACTIVITY

Reflect on ways that the feeling of not mattering can impact the way we live. Pray through this activity to see what God might be saying to you and what unexpected insights might arise. How do feelings of not mattering impact...

People in the broader culture?

Other people in your life (family, friends, coworkers, neighbors)?

Your own life?

_____

_____

_____

_____

_____

_____

_____

_____

_____

_____

_____

_____

_____

_____

_____

_____

_____

_____

PRAYER ACTIVITY

In this activity, you will read the passage slowly four times. Many find it helpful to read it aloud. After the first reading, answer the first question. After the second reading, the second question. After the third reading, the third question, and after the fourth time of reading it, answer the fourth question. The passage for this activity is Psalm 139:13-18.

Question #1: What stands out to you? Don't think about this; just jot down what you see.

_____

_____

_____

_____

_____

_____

_____

_____

Question #2: Is there anything that stirs your heart as you read the passage a second time? If so, write it down.

_____

_____

_____

_____

_____

_____

_____

_____

Question #3: How can you express what you see in this passage into a prayer? Do that now.

_____

_____

_____

_____

_____

_____

_____

Question #4: What do you sense God is saying to you?

_____

_____

_____

_____

_____

_____

_____

_____

_____

_____

_____

_____

_____

RELATIONSHIP ACTIVITY

Pray for the people in your group. Ask the Lord to show you a unique way how to express to another person how they matter. Send an email or a card or reach out on the phone simply to express you have been praying for them. Just try it and see what God might do through your efforts.

_____

_____

_____

_____

_____

_____

_____

_____

_____

_____

_____

_____

_____

_____

_____

_____

_____

_____

_____

_____

_____

YOUR WORKMANSHIP IS MARVELOUS

-Psalm 139:13-14

WEEK 1/DAY 1

Psalm 139: 13-18 NLT

Our search for meaning and purpose inevitable leads us to our Creator. He has not only designed and molded our being, but He's also breathed His breath and dignity into our existence. To try to understand ourselves and our worth while excluding God will only lead to despair.

When we see ourselves within God's plan and purposes, then we find true inner peace and fulfillment.

King David's words in Psalm 139 are honest, introspective and blunt. We may deceive ourselves, but God knows us all too well. In fact, He knows us better than we know ourselves. He knows our story from beginning to end. He thought of us, formed us and loved us even when we were in the womb. Every day of our life, before birth and up to death, is laid out before our Creator. He is not a distant engineer. He is a marvelous artist with precious plans and purposes scripted into our story. Whether we sleep or are awake, not only does His plan unfold, but He is actually there with us.

A true understanding of life always keeps the gift of life in perspective. When we see ourselves through the lens of His love and purpose, everything else becomes clear. Our worries, obstacles and fears no longer eclipse our sight. Our faith and confidence in Him strengthens hope in the deepest part of our soul. We see Him. Through Him, we see ourselves. We remember that we are loved. We are meaningful. We have purpose. We have destiny.

PRAYER: Lord, remind me daily how much You love me. Remind me that You've known me for longer than I've known myself. Help me remember that You have a plan that is still unfolding in my life. Don't let me lose sight of Your purposes, and above all things, never let me lose sight of You.

NOTES

WEEK 1/DAY 2

Jeremiah 1:4-8 NLT

We can easily find ourselves going into autopilot and letting life run its course, forgetting about the divine purpose that was knit together so intricately in the unique fibers of our being. Distractions, insecurities, low self-esteem, fear of failure, selfish ambitions... these are just some of the many things that can throw us off our God-destined course, but it's never too late to get back on track. God is here with us now and He is ready to lead each one of us into our destiny.

In this passage of scripture, the prophet Jeremiah heard God's call on his life but tried to shy away from it by bringing up his youth. Jeremiah told God that he couldn't speak for Him because of his young age. I think Jeremiah wasn't just insecure about being too young to be used by God; he may have had the real fear of missing out on his years of youth. He may have also feared traveling out of his town... but God redirected him and made Jeremiah a promise to be with him, giving him the right words to say and leading him to the right places at the right times. God's purpose and plan on Jeremiah's life was already spoken into existence even before he was born or conceived. God's purpose will always be greater than what our flesh can handle; that's why we need His strength and guidance each step of the way.

Think about it like this: God made the physical you for the purpose He has for you. He made you on purpose!

No mistake can erase the God-given purpose on your life.

There's nothing in this world that can rob you of that divine purpose that is supernaturally woven into your DNA. Turn towards God; listen for His voice. Let Him guide you and reveal the next step on your purpose journey. You were born for this!

PRAYER: Lord, help me learn to hear Your voice and not to allow my flesh to get in the way. May I eagerly follow You and seek Your purpose for my life.

NOTES

_____

_____

_____

_____

_____

_____

_____

_____

_____

_____

_____

_____

_____

_____

_____

_____

_____

_____

_____

_____

_____

_____

WEEK 1/DAY 3

Luke 1:8-17 NLT

One of the greatest times of the year in Minnesota is late spring / early summer. Yes, the change in weather is welcomed. Yes, that signals the beginning of "cabin season." However, I love this time of year in Minnesota for another reason... it's grad party season! It is so fun going from party to party celebrating the accomplishments of students while also eating amazing food! During these parties, the same topic always comes up while speaking with the student who just graduated. "What are you going to do next?"

Hidden within that question is the same question we often ask ourselves, no matter the age: "What is my purpose?"

Purpose is the treasure that we all have been in search of since we were young, and yet still have such a difficult time obtaining.

We look for it in relationships, whether they be romantic or friendly. We search for purpose in our relationships with our children. One of the most common places we tend to assume we will find our purpose is within our occupation. We tend to believe that the place we receive a paycheck is the same source of our purpose. Yet all these places will let us down one way or another.

Purpose cannot be found in a person or a place. Purpose is found within a posture. Pastor Nate likes to say, "We are not called to a profession or a paycheck; we are called to faithfulness." We see this demonstrated in Luke 1:8-17. There we meet a priest named Zechariah and his wife, Elizabeth, who is unable to conceive a child. Verse 6 tells us that they were "righteous in the sight of God, observing all the Lord's commands and decrees blamelessly." During a season of great pain and shame for not being able to conceive a child, they remained in a posture of faithfulness. They could have used their situation as an excuse to be angry with God, to

19

question His plan or even His love, but Zechariah and Elizabeth remained faithful.

In spite of his pain, Zechariah kept showing up to work. He kept showing up to the place that was built to honor and glorify the same God that had allowed them to be barren. That is such a powerful action. Zechariah chose to worship the same God that allowed his greatest pain to exist. Zechariah knew that He was called to faithfulness, and faithfulness is not contingent upon a season; it is consistent in all seasons. There in the sanctuary, in his faithfulness, is where God met him with his purpose.

Be encouraged that the Lord sees you. Even when you feel alone, in pain and questioning your purpose, know that He has something in store for you. You do not need to go in search of your purpose as if it was some hidden treasure for you to find. Your purpose is found within your posture. When you choose the posture of faithfulness, God will meet you where you are with something grander that you could ever imagine!

PRAYER: Lord, help me to be faithful to follow You, even when pain is present. I will not use my situation as an excuse to be angry. I will find ways to trust You and remain in a posture of worship and reverence in every season of life.

NOTES

_____

_____

_____

_____

_____

_____

_____

_____

WEEK 1/DAY 4

Ephesians 2:8-10 NLT

"What do you do?" The first time you have a conversation with a person, this is one of the first questions asked. Our culture puts so much emphasis on what we do. It can be a bit lazy or perhaps guarded, as if we can get all the information we need about someone by what they do. While what you do is important, who you are matters so much more.

God loves you so much He sent His only Son, Jesus, to save you. It is a gift that cost Him everything, and He is asking you to believe and accept His gift. There is nothing you can do to earn your salvation. No amount of good works or "perfect" living can save you. Otherwise, as Paul states, you would have something to brag about. Similarly, no amount of sin is too great for God and His grace. Jesus overcame all sin and offers freedom and new life in Him.

His grace is not a reward; it is a gift.

You are God's masterpiece! Think on that for a moment. God declares you a masterpiece. You have a great purpose with a lifetime of missions and the empowerment to accomplish all God set out for you to do. That's right: God created you with a master plan to DO good things! God loves you so much He not only wanted to save you, but He prepared a plan for you before you were born to represent Him and accomplish good things. We are not saved by works but FOR works – to have Kingdom impact in the world around us!

You were born to be on mission – to do! I encourage you, not to let the routine of life control your day or to be defined by your vocation, but to focus on who you are in Him and to accomplish the good things He has planned for you to do!

Are you on mission? Today and this week, how can you bring Christ's light, hope and love to your family, workplace, neighborhood, school, community and everywhere you go?

PRAYER: Lord, thank You for the gift of Your grace and salvation. Help me see myself as You see me, a masterpiece with a plan and a purpose to do good things. Lead and guide me. Help me stay on mission to impact this world for You and Your kingdom. Your kingdom come; Your will be done, on earth as it is in heaven.

NOTES

WEEK 1/DAY 5

Phillipians 3:12-16 NLT

The year was 1929. Roy Riegels desperately wanted his team to win the Rose Bowl. A fumble occurred and Roy scooped up the loose ball and started running. He cut in and out of traffic, eluding tacklers with breathtaking athleticism. He sprinted the distance of the field. He ran to the 30, to the 20, to the 10, to the 5, and then was tackled by his own teammate and then members of the opposing team. He was stopped one yard shy of the goal line.

Why did his teammate stop him? Because Roy Riegels had lost his bearings and run the wrong way. For the rest of his life, he was not known for his remarkable athletic abilities. He was known as Roy the "Wrong Way" Riegels.

This blunder made Riegels a better person and he used it as a catapult to help others develop a strong forward focus to keep going.

In our scripture, Paul made knowing Christ the most important thing in his life. Paul clarifies he had not already obtained all this; he had not already been made perfect. He let this truth motivate him to press on towards God's goal for his life.

The Bible compares the Christian life to a race. There are different types of races, and the Christian life is best compared to a marathon. It is not a 100-yard dash, and it is most definitely not a walk in the park. It is a daily challenge that requires focus, effort and perseverance to overcome the obstacles in your way.

We are long-distance runners who require a strong forward focus to keep going, and we need to run with the right destination in mind.

Today, ensure that you are pursuing God and His will. Focus on His activity and action in your life. Look for His direction and His purposes. Look to build your life on faith rather than certainty. You may be experiencing a "wrong way" moment in your life, but be encouraged to keep moving forward. God will refresh you for your tomorrow.

PRAYER: Lord, help me to focus on Your activity in my life. Give me strength to keep going so I may experience Your plans and purposes for my life each day.

NOTES

_____

_____

_____

_____

_____

_____

_____

_____

_____

_____

_____

_____

_____

_____

_____

_____

_____

_____

_____

SESSION 2:
ROOM FOR THIS

SCRIPTURE MEMORY:

"Seek the Kingdom of God above all else, and live righteously, and he will give you everything you need."

– Matthew 6:33 NLT

WELCOME

Give one another five to ten minutes to arrive and get settled in. If possible, provide light snacks and have upbeat music playing in the background.

CHECKING IN

ASK: Which of the following two options describe you better: messy bedroom or organized bedroom? Why do you say that?

WATCH: PLAY SESSION 2A OF THIS MATTERS VIDEO SERIES AND WRITE DOWN ANYTHING THAT STANDS OUT TO YOU FROM THE TEACHING.

_____

_____

_____

_____

_____

_____

_____

_____

_____

_____

_____

_____

_____

_____

_____

_____

_____

_____

_____

_____

_____

_____

GROUP DISCUSSION QUESTIONS

#1 READ ALOUD: In the video teaching, Pastor Nate expressed how it is common for us to add so many things to our plate that we get to the point where we cannot handle it any more.

> **ASK:** What happens to us emotionally and spiritually when this occurs?

#2 READ ALOUD: Matthew 6:31-33 NLT

> **ASK:** How does worrying about all the things on our plate hinder our walk with God?

> **ASK:** According to this passage, what is the alternative to worry? What does it mean to seek first the kingdom of God?

#3 READ ALOUD: Pastor Nate talked about the difference between spending and investing.

> **ASK:** How does "spending" starve your life? How does "investing" feed your life?

#4 READ ALOUD: The Bible provides some basic guidelines so that we can learn to practice seeking first the kingdom. These guidelines involve practicing the Sabbath, prioritizing our abilities and talents, and giving our finances to God.

> **ASK:** How might you implement the principle of "Rest 1 day, Run 6 days"?

> **ASK:** What can you do to take your abilities and talents to the next level?

> **ASK:** What is God saying to you about your finances?

#5 READ OUT LOUD: Some people find it overwhelming to discuss how their plate is too full. In fact, for some it is paralyzing. Just know that we can be here for one another as we learn together how God might be leading us in a new direction. We don't have to try and fix this in isolation. In fact, we can pray for one another about these things right now.

WORSHIP AND PRAYER TIME

PRAYER REQUESTS: Ask for everyone's prayer requests. Encourage everyone to share their requests briefly so you can spend more time praying for your requests than talking about them. Be sure to record them on the Small Group Prayer and Praise Report on pages 140-141 of this study guide. Commit to pray for each other's requests every day of the week. Once all the requests are gathered, move into a group worship time.

GROUP WORSHIP AND PRAYER TIME:

Before you pray for each other, invite the presence of the Lord into your time by playing the worship video for this week (Session 2B). As the worship time concludes, flow into your time of prayer by praying over the prayer requests. Encourage the group to participate by praying for one of the prayer requests that were listed.

DISMISSAL

- Talk about the next group meeting.
- Encourage each other to continue to pray for each other throughout the week.
- Encourage group members to invite anyone they think will benefit from being in the group to the next meeting.
- Add any new person to the Small Group Roster on page 139 of this study guide.

JOURNALING ACTIVITY

Use the following chart to reflect on the last week and how you spent your time. You don't need to include details; just list what you did during the morning, afternoon, and evening. Try to list the people you engaged with in those activities. Think through the following:

	MORNING	AFTERNOON	EVENING
DAY 1			
DAY 2			
DAY 3			
DAY 4			
DAY 5			
DAY 6			
DAY 7			

- What does this say about how full your plate is?
- What does this say about your priorities?
- When might you be able to practice the Sabbath in your weekly schedule?
- Pray and be open to what the Lord might show you.

PRAYER ACTIVITY

In this activity, you will read the passage slowly four times. Many find it helpful to read it aloud. After the first reading, answer the first question. After the second reading, the second question. After the third reading, the third question, and after the fourth time of reading it, answer the fourth question. The passage for this activity is Matthew 6:31-33 NLT.

Try doing this activity with the same passage over multiple days. You will see new things each time.

Question #1: What stands out to you? Don't think about this; just jot down what you see.

_____

_____

_____

_____

_____

_____

Question #2: Is there anything that stirs your heart as you read the passage a second time? If so, write it down.

_____

_____

_____

_____

_____

_____

_____

Question #3: How can you express what you see in this passage into a prayer? Do that now.

_____

_____

_____

_____

_____

_____

_____

Question #4: What do you sense God is saying to you?

_____

_____

_____

_____

_____

_____

_____

_____

_____

_____

_____

_____

_____

_____

_____

RELATIONSHIP ACTIVITY

Review your week and see how you can make a friend from your group
a priority outside of the meeting time. Reach out to someone and see if
you can meet up for coffee, go for a walk, or do something that you both
enjoy. It need not be significant; keep it simple and let the Spirit work
through you.

_____

_____

_____

_____

_____

_____

_____

_____

_____

_____

_____

_____

_____

_____

_____

_____

_____

_____

SEEK THE KINGOM OF —— GOD —— ABOVE ALL ELSE

-Matthew 6:33

WEEK 2/DAY 1

Proverbs 3:5-10 NLT

C.S. Lewis once wrote in Mere Christianity about the process we go through when God enters our life. He wrote:

Imagine yourself as a living house. God comes in to rebuild that house. At first, perhaps, you can understand what He is doing. He is getting the drains right and stopping the leaks in the roof and so on; you knew that those jobs needed doing and so you are not surprised. But presently He starts knocking the house about in a way that hurts abominably and does not seem to make any sense. What on earth is He up to? The explanation is that He is building quite a different house from the one you thought of - throwing out a new wing here, putting on an extra floor there, running up towers, making courtyards.

You thought you were being made into a decent little cottage: but He is building a palace. He intends to come and live in it Himself.

As you approach your day today, think about what it is to trust God with everything that you are, to seek Him in everything that you do and to honor Him with everything that you have.

Proverbs teaches us that if we trust Him with our whole heart and seek Him in everything that we do, He will lead us to the right pathway. It also tells us that if we honor God with everything we have, our wealth, that He will provide for us to a point of overflowing.

I love this portion of Proverbs because all of the things we typically worry about in life, God tells us that He will take care of for us. We simply need to trust, seek and honor Him.

PRAYER: Lord, thank You for Your mindfulness of us. This proverb shows us that You provide everything we need. Help us to embrace this truth. Help us to lean into Your word and Your Spirit today.

NOTES

WEEK 2/DAY 2

Matthew 6:19-24 NLT

We live in a day and age of obsessive materialism and if we're not careful, we can be swept away with the trends. In Matthew 6:19-24, Jesus presented a paradigm shift. He showed us the way we approach our earthly treasure can directly impact our legacy, our identity and our faith in God.

"Don't store up treasures here on earth, where moths eat them and rust destroys them, and where thieves break in and steal. Store your treasures in heaven, where moths and rust cannot destroy, and thieves do not break in and steal" (Matthew 6:19-20 NLT). Hoarding as much as we can here on earth is a temporary pursuit with temporary gains that eventually perish. When we live each day for heaven's purposes instead of living each day for money, we begin to build an eternal legacy that will be imperishable.

"Wherever your treasure is, there the desires of your heart will also be" (Matthew 6:21 NLT). Our inner man is hidden to others but not to God. Jesus sees the true condition of our hearts and what we treasure determines its quality. Selfishness and greed produce an ugly heart before God while living with purpose according to what matters most cultivates an inner beauty that pleases heaven.

> *"No one can serve two masters. For you will hate one and love the other; you will be devoted to one and despise the other. You cannot serve God and be enslaved to money."*
> *- Matthew 6:24 NLT*

Rick Warren says, *"Money has the greatest potential to replace God in your life."* We can live to become wealth builders or kingdom builders, but both cannot matter the most. Which one matters more in your life today? Living each day for God's kingdom results in you storing up an eternal inheritance, cultivating a healthy inner man and laboring to see heaven here on earth.

PRAYER: Lord, help me to seek You above all else today. I am available to be unselfish, generous and used by You in the lives of others.

NOTES

_____

_____

_____

_____

_____

_____

_____

_____

_____

_____

_____

_____

_____

_____

_____

_____

_____

_____

_____

_____

_____

_____

_____

_____

_____

_____

_____

WEEK 2/DAY 3

Matthew 6:25-34 NLT

When it comes to making room for the things that matter in our lives, there is a very odd, yet real tension most of us wrestle with on a daily basis. Why is it the things we say matter most are usually the things that show up last? Talking about your priorities and living out what you prioritize are two different things.

A major obstacle for us in this tension is worry. What we worry about is not usually what is happening to me but whether what is in me is strong enough to handle what happens to me.

Think about what keeps us up at night: finances, kids, work, deadlines, car problems, house projects. The list can go on and on. In Matthew 6:25-34, Jesus uses a great illustration to point us to some healthy habits on how to navigate the tension of worry and begin to make room for His peace.

He uses an illustration of a bird and a flower to highlight their lack of worry from day to day. Their secret?

-Stay above it.
-Stay planted.

> *We protect what we prize; peace should be important to us! The only way to live in God's peace is to have God's priorities. Every time there is a lack of peace, it comes back to priorities.*

The presence of problems does not mean an absence of peace and the absence of problems does not mean we have peace. Problems help us clarify our priorities.

In seventeenth century France, a humble church leader named Fénelon wrote a letter of encouragement to believers who sought spiritual perspective during some discouraging trials. He said, Do not worry about the future. It makes no sense to worry if God loves you and has taken care of you. However, when God blesses you, remember to keep your eyes on Him and not the blessing.

When worry begins to take up too much room from what matters, let us learn from the sparrow and the flower:

Stay above it (have peace).
Stay rooted (trust God).

PRAYER: Lord, when worry tries to take up space in my life from the things that matter, help me stay above the worry, rooted in You.

NOTES

_____

_____

_____

_____

_____

_____

_____

_____

_____

_____

_____

_____

_____

WEEK 2/DAY 4

Ephesians 5:15-20 NLT

God has uniquely created each of us and He has given us a place to express that uniqueness. However, at times, we can get so caught up in the "mission" or the "calling" that we forget to live each day to the fullest.

I sometimes miss the simple opportunities that come daily where I can be the hands and feet of Christ to the world around me. I believe this is partly what Paul is talking about in this passage in Ephesians. We are to be careful, maybe even watchful, about the way we live. We are to "make the most of every opportunity," not acting foolishly, but acting out of wisdom. We are to "understand what the Lord wants you to do" and then be obedient and do those things. Here is where purpose lives.

Are we doing the things God wants us to do?

Some of those things are ordinary things like being kind, meeting the needs of people around us, encouraging others, listening to people, providing a meal, lending a hand or helping someone move. Some of those things are directly related to our God-given design, His call on our lives. Possibly the list contains things we should not engage in like gossip, judgment, criticism, envy, jealousy. Whichever category, we are to embrace the opportunity, acting with wisdom as we carry out the task.

None of this comes easily. We need God's help and we need one another! I am so grateful that the Holy Spirit equips us with everything we need. So, instead of worrying and fretting, let's discipline ourselves to be filled with the Spirit, allowing the songs of thanksgiving to come from within us. Then we will have the power to live wise, fruitful lives as we accomplish what the Lord asks of us.

PRAYER: Lord, thank You for being with me. I know that You are! Help me to live wisely, to not miss opportunities that You give me to see You at work in my life and the world around me. Equip me to be able to understand what You want me to do and then to have the capacity to be obedient and do those things.

NOTES

_____

_____

_____

_____

_____

_____

_____

_____

_____

_____

_____

_____

_____

_____

_____

_____

_____

_____

_____

_____

_____

WEEK 2/DAY 5

Phillipians 4:10-20 NLT

Often times we can get so caught up in our jobs, school, family, running the kids around, trying to make a living that we forget why we are here! Much of today's culture tells us that we need more! We need a better job. We need a bigger house. We need more "likes" or "views." We end up filling our schedules with so much "doing" that we forget to just "be." I know in my own life that this is something I have to fight against.

Now hear me out, wanting something better in your life isn't necessarily bad. It's the thought process of "I never have enough" that can be destructive.

Here, Paul is talking about being content in all seasons and situations. Whether we have a job we love, a job that is really tough, or maybe we are just trying to make ends meet. Paul teaches us through his words and actions that we can be content in whatever season with whatever we have.

Contentment isn't ever found in physical things.

He says in verses 12 and 13, "I know how to live on almost nothing or with everything. I have learned the secret of living in every situation, whether it is with a full stomach or empty, with plenty or little. For I can do everything through Christ, who gives me strength."

Paul tells us the secret to being content in everything. It's Jesus! Christ is the one who gives strength in the hard times and Christ is the one who gives us strength in the good times! It is in Christ that we find our peace, our hope and our strength. All that we need can be found in Him and when we find Him, meet with Him and have a relationship with Him, that is when we will find contentment.

PRAYER: Lord, I am so thankful for everything that You have blessed me with. Help me to be content in all circumstances. Show me what that looks like and how to live a life of contentment. Thank You for being my strength!

NOTES

_____

_____

_____

_____

_____

_____

_____

_____

_____

_____

_____

_____

_____

_____

_____

_____

_____

_____

_____

_____

SESSION 3:
FAMILY MATTERS

SCRIPTURE MEMORY:

"But as for me and my house, we will serve the Lord."

–Joshua 24:15, NLT

WELCOME

Give one another five to ten minutes to arrive and get settled in.
If possible, provide light snacks and have upbeat music playing
in the background.

CHECKING IN

ASK: What is something fun you have done since we last met?

 **PLAY SESSION 3A OF THIS MATTERS VIDEO SERIES AND WRITE DOWN ANYTHING THAT STANDS OUT TO YOU FROM THE TEACHING.**

GROUP DISCUSSION QUESTIONS

#1 READ OUT LOUD: Talking about family is a sensitive subject. Some of us might be experiencing family stress as we speak. Do not feel the pressure to reveal anything that you don't feel comfortable sharing. At the same time, do not feel the pressure to pretend that your family situation is perfect. We have all been there.

> **ASK:** How can our family situation impact our service to God, for good or for bad?

> **READ ALOUD:** Pastor Nate mentioned the importance of our vision for the future of our family. Why is our vision so crucial? How can our previous experiences of family (our family of origin) impact our vision?

#2 READ ALOUD: Joshua 24:15: "But as for me and my house, we will serve the Lord." (ESV)

> **ASK:** What is the significance that this verse starts with "me"? What difference can the resolve of one person make in your family?

#3 READ OUT LOUD: The reference to "my house" entails everything that is under your influence.

> **ASK:** What does it mean to commit those things to the Lord?

> **ASK:** What does is mean for you to serve the Lord in the midst of your family? What needs to change?

#4 READ ALOUD: Time is crucial to our family life. If we don't invest time and energy there, we will not reap the reward of healthy relationships with one another.

> **ASK:** Why is time so important to a healthy family?

> **ASK:** How has the joy of your family risen or fallen according to the amount of time you invest in one another? What does this tell you regarding your priorities, especially in light of the conversation from last week?

WORSHIP AND PRAYER TIME

PRAYER REQUESTS: Ask for everyone's prayer requests.
Encourage everyone to share their requests briefly so you can
spend more time praying for your requests than talking about
them. Be sure to record them on the Small Group Prayer and Praise
Report on pages 140-141 of this study guide. Commit to pray for
each other's requests every day of the week. Once all the requests
are gathered, move into a group worship time.

GROUP WORSHIP TIME:

Before you pray for each other, invite the presence
of the Lord into your time by playing the worship
video for this week (Session 3B). As the worship
time concludes, flow into your time of prayer by
praying over the prayer requests. Encourage the
group to participate by praying for one of the
prayer requests that were listed.

DISMISSAL

- Talk about the next group meeting.
- Encourage each other to continue to pray for each other
  throughout the week.
- Encourage group members to invite anyone they think will benefit
  from being in the group to the next meeting.
- Add any new person to the Small Group Roster on page 139 of this
  study guide.

JOURNALING ACTIVITY

Based on the teaching of family of origin, how has your experience of family resulted in patterns that you would like to see changed?

_____

_____

_____

_____

_____

_____

_____

_____

_____

_____

_____

_____

_____

How has your family of origin influenced your patterns in a positive way?

_____

_____

_____

_____

_____

_____

_____

_____

_____

_____

_____

_____

_____

Spend some time offering both the negative and positive to the Lord, listening to the Spirit as you do so.

_____

_____

_____

_____

_____

_____

_____

_____

_____

_____

_____

_____

_____

_____

_____

PRAYER ACTIVITY

In this activity, you will read the passage slowly four times. Many find it helpful to read it aloud. After the first reading, answer the first question. After the second reading, the second question. After the third reading, the third question, and after the fourth time of reading it, answer the fourth question. The passage for this activity is Joshua 24:14-15.

Question #1: What stands out to you? Don't think about this; just jot down what you see.

_____

_____

_____

_____

_____

_____

_____

_____

Question #2: Is there anything that stirs your heart as you read the passage a second time? If so, write it down.

_____

_____

_____

_____

_____

_____

_____

Question #3: How can you express what you see in this passage into a prayer? Do that now.

_____

_____

_____

_____

_____

_____

_____

Question #4: What do you sense God is saying to you?

_____

_____

_____

_____

_____

_____

_____

_____

_____

_____

_____

_____

_____

_____

_____

RELATIONSHIP ACTIVITY

Plan an activity to do with someone in your family that breaks the
routine. For instance, take your spouse on a date, if that is not a common
pattern. Take your kids out to do something they enjoy. Send a card to
your parents, for no reason at all. It might feel unusual at first because
it is not a habit, but the only way to create new habits is to start doing
something new.

BUT AS FOR ME AND MY HOUSEHOLD WE WILL SERVE THE LORD

- Joshua 24:15

WEEK 3/DAY 1

Genesis 2:15-25 NLT

Part of the purpose God wired into humanity is to care for and invest into family. But why does family matter? What makes family so important? Let's look at the first family—Adam and Eve—to glean some insight.

Verse 18 is key: "It is not good for man to be alone." God never intended for us to serve Him or pursue His grand purpose alone. In 1 Corinthians 12, Paul elaborates on God's purpose for us as part of His body. Each one of us is a member of a greater body working together, and Christ is the head. God didn't intend for us to be loners or lonely! He knew if we were alone, we would be vulnerable.

So how does God solve the problem? He created Eve, a "helper" for man. This word "helper" is the Hebrew noun ezer. Ezer appears 21 times in the Old Testament; 16 of those times, it's used to describe God helping His people. When God took a rib from Adam and formed Eve, He formed the perfect "helper." God didn't create Eve to serve Adam. Eve was created to strengthen Adam like God strengthens His people.

Another form of ezer is the Hebrew verb azer, which can be translated: "to help, to protect, to support, to ally." What an amazing picture! Eve made Adam a better person. Eve protected, supported and allied with Adam. She helped him and they pursued God's purpose together.

Today, I challenge you to pause and thank God for your family.

Thank Him for your spouse, your parents, your children and your spiritual brothers and sisters. Are those relationships making you more like Jesus? Are you making your family more like Jesus? Family is a gift for strength! Let's be like Jesus for each other.

PRAYER: Lord, help me to sow life into my family and offer them my best. I want to embrace Your purpose and I want to do it with the family You've given me for strength! I submit myself to You as the head of our great family.

NOTES

_____
_____
_____
_____
_____
_____
_____
_____
_____
_____
_____
_____
_____
_____
_____
_____
_____
_____
_____
_____
_____
_____
_____
_____

WEEK 3/DAY 2

Ephesians 5:21-33 NLT

This is a powerful passage that is very clear in its call to action. Husbands and wives are shown the biblical roles to which they should strive in their marriage. Wives are to "submit to your husbands as to the Lord." Husbands are to "love your wives, just as Christ loved the church." We are usually comfortable with the prescribed role of the husband to love his wife. Love is naturally associated with marriage, like peanut butter and jelly. But our culture can find issue with the prescribed role of the wife to submit to her husband.

Submission isn't usually something you would associate with marriage, more like snow in July.

Submitting to someone is a very difficult thing to do; and as everyone who is married can attest to, it can be even more difficult to submit to the person you share your life with. When you live in close proximity with someone, you become fully aware of all their flaws. As each flaw becomes apparent, respect becomes more difficult.

One detail that can easily be missed in this passage is at the very beginning, in verse 21, "'And further, submit to one another out of reverence for Christ." This key verse sets the stage for everything else we are called to do within marriage. Both husband and wife are called to submit to one another. The ease or difficulty of submission are usually tied to the situation we find ourselves in. For example, it is easier for me to respect my wife when it comes to preparing food than it is to respect her when it comes to how I drive. In the confines of marriage, situations change and seasons come and go, but we are called to "submit to one another" anyway. This is why verse 21 is so vital. "And further, submit to one another out of reverence for Christ." The key to submitting regardless of the situation is that our submission should come out of respect for Christ, not out of respect (or lack of respect) for our spouse.

My challenge for you today is to live out this verse, "'And further, submit to one another out of reverence for Christ."

PRAYER: Lord, help me submit to my spouse out of my respect for You. Help me love my spouse like You love the church. I ask that today, Your love for my spouse would be made evident through me. Help our marriage be an example of Your love for the church.

NOTES

_____

_____

_____

_____

_____

_____

_____

_____

_____

_____

_____

_____

_____

_____

_____

_____

_____

_____

_____

WEEK 3/DAY 3

Ephesians 6:1-4 NLT

Have you ever been in a relationship that seems very one-sided? You feel like you are giving more than you are receiving. This can be a very frustrating thing to experience and often feels like a losing battle. Sometimes as parents we feel like this with our children, like we are constantly giving and receiving little in return.

When we feel like this and then read something like Ephesians 6:1-4, we can potentially take it the wrong way. Inside we are thinking, "Yeah, you kids obey me and things will go well for you!" The problem is if we get stuck in this very transactional way of viewing relationships, we will miss what the point of relationship is all about. A relationship is to be mutually beneficial, causing one another to grow and change. It is not for the benefit of one individual over the other.

> *Relationships need to be firmly built on a foundation of honor and respect, mutually giving back and forth within the context of healthy boundaries.*

This repeated over time builds trust, which can then be utilized to train and instruct in the ways of the Lord. Verse 4 beautifully states this: "Fathers, do not provoke your children to anger by the way you treat them. Rather, bring them up with the discipline and instruction that comes from the Lord."

Parents all face moments of frustration as we raise up those growing in faith, young or old. Let me encourage you the investment is worth it! We are shown that the Word does not return void, things that are sown will be reaped and there is no greater investment than pouring into your family!

Don't beat yourself up if you feel like you have been failing. Tomorrow is a new day; kids are forgiving and the most important thing is that you are present every day for them.

PRAYER: Lord, I can't do this on my own. I need You! Reveal to me the areas I am provoking my children to anger and forgive me. Give me the grace I need to step up to the responsibility and authority I have as a parent to raise my children in the ways of the Lord.

NOTES

_____

_____

_____

_____

_____

_____

_____

_____

_____

_____

_____

_____

_____

_____

_____

_____

_____

WEEK 3/DAY 4

Psalm 127:3-5 NLT

Reading these verses from Psalm 127 gives us some great reminders and perspective. Whether you are a parent or not, there are two undeniable truths we can take away about children. The first truth is that every child is a gift from God (verse 3). The second truth is that every child has a purpose, or you can say, has a target to hit (verse 4). As parents and leaders, we have to understand the importance of investing in the children in and around our lives as we come to understand these truths. It matters to invest in them spiritually and personally.

As a parent, I understand that God has given me the responsibility to lead my kids, but at times when life hits and things get busy, it is easy for me to invest in everything else except them. I know that can happen to many of us at times.

We can invest so much in other people or other things that we forget to invest in our children.

Verse 4 in this psalm tells us that children are like arrows in a warrior's hand. Allow me to pose this question: What good does an unsharpened arrow do for a warrior? It can still be shot and it can probably still hit its target, but it will not pierce through and leave its mark. To invest in our children is to sharpen our children.

When I reflect on this psalm, what I hear in my heart is, "Investing in our children matters!" My encouragement for you today, whether you are a parent leading your own children or a leader who has the opportunity to lead the children of others, see children's value. See that they have purpose and invest in them. This will help them one day see their value, see that they have purpose and help them leave their mark on the target they are launched toward.

PRAYER: Lord, today I pray that You would help me see the value and the purpose of the children that You have placed in my life. Give me wisdom to teach and patience to guide. Help me to have the courage to correct and the heart to love unconditionally. I submit my life to You so that You can lead me as I lead others.

NOTES

_____

_____

_____

_____

_____

_____

_____

_____

_____

_____

_____

_____

_____

_____

_____

_____

_____

_____

_____

_____

_____

_____

_____

WEEK 3/DAY 5

Joshua 24:14-18 NLT

Serving God is a choice that each of us need to intentionally choose.

If we live by default, the choice will be made for us; we will fall into the temptations offered by the world. It is the same with our family. If we live by default, we will choose to embrace the values of the world for our family. It is so important to intentionally invest time and impart biblical values into the ones we love.

Our society values so many things: money, material things, fame, sports, friendships, personal rights and status. While many of these things are not bad on their own, God's kingdom is different. In God's kingdom the servant is the greatest and people are valued. Love, forgiveness, generosity, prayer, fellowship, spiritual growth and the presence of God are just a few of the things found in the community of believers.

Joshua finds himself addressing the Israelites and offering them a choice – serve the Lord alone or by default you will choose to serve another god. It's one or the other. Joshua declares his choice to the community, "But as for me and my house, we will serve the LORD." (Joshua 24:15b ESV). The Israelites did not realize that being passive meant that they were really choosing to serve another god. When the choice was clarified, they intentionally chose to serve the Lord too!

We need to intentionally chose to serve the Lord with our family and make our intentions clear – we will serve the Lord! Here are a few small ways you can invest biblical values into your family. Do these things together: prioritize church attendance, pray before meals and bedtime, read the Bible aloud and listen to worship music. Eventually our children have to make their own choice to serve the Lord, but we will have planted spiritual seeds in their heart that will grow over time.

PRAYER: Lord, help me to not live by default and not simply follow the world. Help me to be intentional about choosing You with my family so that I can also declare, "but as for me and my house, we will serve the Lord." Please help me plant the seeds of Your Word in the hearts of the next generation so they will have the foundation to choose You as well.

NOTES

SESSION 4:
THIS IS US

SCRIPTURE MEMORY:

"Let us think of ways to motivate one another to acts of love and good works. And let us not neglect our meeting together, as some people do, but encourage one another, especially now that the day of his return is drawing near."

– Hebrews 10:24-25, NLT

WELCOME

Give one another five to ten minutes, to arrive and get settled in. If possible, provide light snacks and have upbeat music playing in the background.

CHECKING IN

ASK: What is a personal church experience/memory that brings a smile to your face?

PLAY SESSION 4A OF THIS MATTERS VIDEO SERIES AND WRITE DOWN ANYTHING THAT STANDS OUT TO YOU FROM THE TEACHING.

GROUP DISCUSSION QUESTIONS

#1 READ ALOUD: Pastor Nate talked about how the RIGHT relationships helped him move closer to the design that Jesus intended for his life and the WRONG friendships took him on detours that benefitted neither him nor his friends.

> **ASK:** Why do you think relationships are so crucial to a Christian's development as a follower of Christ?

#2 READ ALOUD: Galatians 6:2-3 NLT

> **ASK:** What does sharing each other's burdens look like? How have you experienced this in the past?

> **ASK:** How does pride hinder personal growth as a disciple?

#3 READ ALOUD: In the video teaching, the comment was made that our discipleship growth can't happen if everyone in your life is at the same stage as you.

> **ASK:** Why is it important to be in relationship with people who are at different levels of maturity? How can we learn from each other?

> **ASK:** How can this group take a step toward this idea of becoming a set of relationships where we help each other to grow?

#5 READ ALOUD: Tonight we will be sharing communion together as a small group. For some of you, this may be the first time that you have taken communion in a home or in a small group setting. However, in the first churches, they met only in homes in small groups, and this is the way they shared communion. So in that tradition, we are doing what they did. Let's all prepare our hearts to receive the bread and the cup.

> **PASS OUT THE BREAD TO EACH PERSON:** Then **READ ALOUD** Matthew 26:6 NLT: "As they were eating, Jesus took some bread and blessed it. Then he broke it in pieces and gave it to the disciples, saying, "Take this and eat it, for this is my body." ***ALL TAKE THE BREAD.***

> **PASS OUT CUPS OF GRAPE JUICE TO EACH PERSON:** Then **READ ALOUD** Matthew 26:27-28: "And he took a cup of wine and gave thanks to God for it. He gave it to them and said, 'Each of you drink from it, for this is my blood, which confirms the covenant between God and his people. It is poured out as a sacrifice to forgive the sins of many.'" ***ALL DRINK FROM THEIR CUP.***

> **CLOSE IN PRAYER**

WORSHIP AND PRAYER TIME

PRAYER REQUESTS: Ask for everyone's prayer requests. Encourage everyone to share their requests briefly so you can spend more time praying for your requests than talking about them. Be sure to record them on the Small Group Prayer and Praise Report on pages 140-141 of this study guide. Commit to pray for each other's requests every day of the week. Once all the requests are gathered, move into a group worship time.

GROUP WORSHIP AND PRAYER TIME:

Before you pray for each other, invite the presence of the Lord into your time by playing the worship video for this week (Session 4B). As the worship time concludes, flow into your time of prayer by praying over the prayer requests. Encourage the group to participate by praying for one of the prayer requests that were listed.

DISMISSAL

- Talk about the next group meeting.
- Encourage each other to continue to pray for each other throughout the week.

JOURNALING ACTIVITY

Reflect on the close relationships that you have had on your journey.

Identify those who have influenced you to walk with Christ. List them individually and write down a specific way they influenced you. For instance, if Janice, a friend from college, challenged you to read your Bible, write that down. Spend time thanking God for these gifts.

Identify those who have influenced you in ways that are not in alignment with Christ. Identify ways that these patterns continue to impact your life. Maybe you learned some patterns of anger from a good friend ten years ago, something that has continued to this day. Offer these up to God in prayer.

PRAYER ACTIVITY

In this activity, you will read the passage slowly four times. Many find it helpful to read it aloud. After the first reading, answer the first question. After the second reading, the second question. After the third reading, the third question, and after the fourth time of reading it, answer the fourth question. The passage for this activity is Hebrews 10:24-25 NLT.

Question #1: What stands out to you? Don't think about this; just jot down what you see.

_____

_____

_____

_____

_____

_____

_____

_____

Question #2: Is there anything that stirs your heart as you read the passage a second time? If so, write it down.

_____

_____

_____

_____

_____

_____

_____

_____

Question #3: How can you express what you see in this passage into a prayer? Do that now.

_____

_____

_____

_____

_____

_____

_____

_____

Question #4: What do you sense God is saying to you?

_____

_____

_____

_____

_____

_____

_____

_____

_____

_____

_____

_____

_____

_____

RELATIONSHIP ACTIVITY

The Bible tells us to offer hospitality to one another (1 Peter 4:9). Think of a way that you can do this with someone in the group or with the entire group. For instance, you might host a game night for the group. If you enjoy cooking, you might invite another couple over. Someone who enjoys working on cars could offer to work on another member's car, while doing it together. Showing hospitality can also be expressed by inviting someone out for coffee or meeting up for lunch. Ask the Lord to show you a way to make room for other members of the group in your life.

LET US THINK OF WAYS TO MOTIVATE ONE ANOTHER TO ACTS OF LOVE AND GOOD WORKS

- Hebrews 10:24-25

WEEK 4/DAY 1

Matthew 16:13-19 NLT

Defining moments. These are moments that make a lasting impact on the way we view life, the way we live our lives and the person we become. Defining moments shape us. I'm sure you can think of a defining moment that made a great impact on your life. In Matthew 16:13-19, we find Peter in a defining moment of his life.

To give a little context, Peter and the disciples had been a little unsure of Jesus and what He could do. They had been surrounded by the opinions of the Pharisees, Sadducees, and the general public. Even though they had been with Jesus so much, they still had doubts and questions.

Because of this inner battle, this moment that Jesus had with Peter in Matthew 16 was so vital. In this moment, Peter needed to ignore his doubts and the other voices and exercise his faith to declare the truth about Jesus being the Messiah. Once he defined who Jesus was, everything changed for him.

In that moment, Jesus changed Peter's name from Simon to Peter. In that moment, Jesus gave Peter identity and purpose, and as we follow Peter's life in the New Testament, we see him carry out that purpose as he became a leader and a builder of God's Church (the body of Christ). This was a defining moment for Peter that fueled the rest of His life.

Just like Peter had this moment with Jesus, I believe there are moments like this for all of us. Moments when we discover who Jesus is and declare Him as the truth for our lives. That's when everything changes. That's when we find our identity, purpose, strength and life. That's when we step onto the solid foundation of Christ that no force or voices of this world can tear down or stand against.

Peter had a moment like this, but have you? Have you declared that Jesus is Lord? Have you shut out the doubts and other voices, and chosen to live by faith in Him? If not, there's no better day than today to do so. And if you have already done so, how has Jesus changed your life?

Being founded in Him should cause ripple effects in your life and in the lives of others, just like it did for Peter.

PRAYER: *Lord, I silence my doubts and shut out the voices around me, and I declare that You are the Son of God and Savior of the world. Today, I put my faith in who You are and want to become more deeply rooted in Your truth. Let my life be changed by You and impact those with whom I come in contact.*

NOTES

WEEK 4/DAY 2

Ephesians 5:21-33 NLT

I remember the first time I heard this passage. That day and many days since, I have spent lots of time and energy comparing my gifts and strengths to everyone else's. I find myself focused on what gift I wish I had or the gift that someone else had, completely oblivious to the gift that I have been given.

Have you ever been there? Caught yourself thinking "if only I could do _____ like that person over there, then I would feel like I matter and I can make a difference."

***So often, we equate a gift with a position.
So often, we value those gifts based on how
important that position appears to be in
practice.***

Every single one of us has a part to play in the story that God is writing. That story would be incomplete if one of us decided that we were less important than someone else and didn't engage with our gift.

You have a gift. Even if you don't feel like you fit into one of the roles of apostle, prophet, evangelist or pastor, this text also says that God's people are to be equipped to do God's work and build up the church. So no matter who you are or how qualified you feel, you have a role that we need you to step into.

It can be scary and sometimes intimidating, but Christ is the one who equipped you with the gift in the first place and He can be trusted to produce the results. Our responsibility is to simply use our gift.

Your gift has a purpose. God's designed plan is for you to use your gifts for the benefit and building up of those around you. Being a part of the church and using the gifts with which God has equipped you to benefit those you are in relationship with is a key to living with purpose.

What gift have you been given? What can you do today to use that gift to build up the Church?

PRAYER: Lord, help me today to recognize and lean into the gifts You have given me. Give me the courage to take steps into using those gifts and help me live my life to the fullest purpose possible as I trust You with the results.

NOTES

___

___

___

___

___

___

___

___

___

___

___

___

___

___

___

___

___

___

WEEK 4/DAY 3

1 Corinthians 12:12-27 NLT

As we continue to make room for the things that matter in our life, it does not take long to realize the need for strong community. We grow through healthy relationships. We discover purpose in godly community. In our text today, we are reminded that we are one body with many parts. A very real tension that we face is when we are unaware and oblivious to the needs and hurt of other members of the body.

Let's call this spiritual leprosy.

Typical symptoms of leprosy that develop include inflammation of the nerves, respiratory tract, skin and eyes. This may result in a lack of ability to feel pain, thus loss of parts of extremities due to repeated injuries or infection due to unnoticed wounds.

Jesus talks about in John 13 that others would know that we are followers of Christ by how we love one another. As we seek to grow in our ability to love one another, may we not be so numb to the pains of the rest of the body of Christ that we unintentionally cut them off as if we have a form of spiritual leprosy.

That's not what Jesus died for.
That's not the body of Christ.

The only way to be able to know what's going on in the body is to be connected to the body.
Today's challenge may be as simple as asking your coworker how they are doing and caring enough to listen. It may be a text message to that person the Holy Spirit has been prompting you to reach out to and see what's been going on in their life.

Community
Connection
Compassion

This is us.
This is the Church Jesus died for.

PRAYER: Lord, open my spiritual eyes to see others the way that You see them. May the Holy Spirit prompt me to reach out to those who are in need. I want to follow Your heart and not my fears or doubts in loving those around me today!

NOTES

WEEK 4/DAY 4

Romans 12:3-10 NLT

What a beautiful depiction of the church! I love that the body of Christ is diverse, creative and unique. We are one body with many parts. Each part is special and needed. Have you ever felt like you didn't know where you fit in? Have you ever wondered about the God-given gifts that this passage of scripture talks about? God, in His great faithfulness, has given you gifts and He desires for you to function in them as you serve Him and love the people around you.

When you look at your physical body you get the best picture of what the body of Christ is like. Your body is made up of many parts and each part has a specific purpose. The Bible says that it is the same with Christ's body. We are many parts and we all belong to each other. If one part hurts, we all hurt with it. If one part is honored, we all get to rejoice with it. I love that about having community with other believers. We get to walk this journey of faith, linking arms with one another.

It's an amazing thing to be a part of the body of Christ.

Another way in which we work together as the body is by functioning in the gifts that God has given us. Scripture says that whatever gifts you've been given, use them well! If it's serving, serve well. If it's encouraging, then encourage others! I love the simplicity of it. So often we can get caught up in looking at the gifts that others have and wishing we could have the same. The truth is, we need all of the gifts working in harmony with each other to do the mission that God has set before us. I can only imagine the joy that God has when He sees His people honoring Him and one another by allowing the natural gifts to flow out of our lives, bringing the love and hope of Jesus to those who need it.

If you need a reminder of the gifts that He's given you, I encourage you to take a few moments today and spend time with Jesus. Ask Him to renew your heart and to, once again, help you find the simple joy in serving Him. It is a delight when we are flowing in the gifts that He's given. Striving ceases. Comparison fades away. It's like a breath of fresh air for our own lives that helps spur others on to pursue the gifts in their lives as well!

PRAYER: *Lord, my heart's desire is to know You and to be a light that guides people to You. Thank You for Your good gifts and for community with other believers. It is a privilege to honor You and the people around me. Keep me close to Your heart and let everything I say and do be full of genuine love.*

NOTES

_____
_____
_____
_____
_____
_____
_____
_____
_____
_____
_____
_____
_____
_____
_____
_____

WEEK 4/DAY 5

1 John 2:7-17 NLT

Years before this scripture, when Jesus was asked what was the most important commandment of all, Jesus replied, "The most important commandment is this: 'Listen, O Israel! The Lord our God is the one and only Lord. And you must love the Lord your God with all your heart, all your soul, all your mind, and all your strength.' The second is equally important: 'Love your neighbor as yourself.' No other commandment is greater than these." (Mark 12:29-31 NLT)

John is urging the believers to continue loving each other. He is telling them something they already knew. However, John is explaining this old command with a new perspective. He has been encouraging them to live in the light since Jesus is the light. The point he is making in these verses is that living in the light of Christ also means that we will love one another. Jesus modeled what it means to live a life of love, and we are to simply follow His example by loving each other. Jesus demonstrated the greatest kind of love possible when He willingly laid down His life for us. There is no greater love!

Loving each other with that same intensity is not just being willing to die for someone, because that may never be asked of us. However, to lay down our lives is to submit ourselves for the good of someone else, to put their needs or desires before ours and to give unselfishly of ourselves to them for the sake of Christ. We rejoice in their successes and mourn when they mourn.

> *To love means that our lives are not all about ourselves, but through our all-encompassing love for Christ, we extend His love to the very ones He loves.*

Of course, that means everyone!

PRAYER: Lord, fill me today with the capacity to love and help me to extend Your love to everyone around me.

NOTES

SESSION 5:
THE OFFICE (MATTERS)

SCRIPTURE MEMORY:

"You are the salt of the earth. But what good is salt if it has lost
its flavor? Can you make it salty again? It will be thrown out and
trampled underfoot as worthless. You are the light of the world—like a
city on a hilltop that cannot be hidden."

– Matthew 5:13-14, NLT

WELCOME

Give one another five to ten minutes to arrive and get settled in.
If possible, provide light snacks and have upbeat music playing
in the background.

CHECKING IN

ASK: Last week, we talked about how community is connected to
discipleship. How are the relationships in this group impacting you?

PLAY SESSION 5A OF THIS MATTERS VIDEO SERIES AND WRITE DOWN ANYTHING THAT STANDS OUT TO YOU FROM THE TEACHING.

_____

_____

_____

_____

_____

_____

_____

_____

_____

_____

_____

_____

_____

_____

_____

_____

_____

_____

_____

_____

_____

_____

_____

_____

GROUP DISCUSSION QUESTIONS

#1 READ ALOUD: If we spend about one-half of our waking hours on our occupation, then it is important to think about how God views work. Take about five minutes to fill out the following self-assessment.

Rate how much you consciously consider God's involvement in your work.

None   Every day

Rate the attitude you have toward your work.

Negative   Positive

Rate how much you focus on opportunities.

Never   All the time

Rate how much you focus on what you can contribute, not what you can get.

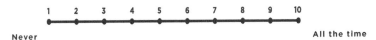

What you can get   What you can contribute

Rate the degree to which you see your job as a place of God's mission.

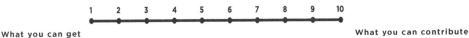

Low   High

After people have had an opportunity to complete this exercise individually, ask: What stands out to you from your responses?

#2 READ ALOUD: Colossians 3:23

ASK: What does this passage teach us about the way we do our work?

#3 READ ALOUD: Pastor Nate talked about three ways to make the office matter. The first is seeing the workplace as an opportunity, not a problem.

> **ASK:** How does a negative view of work dominate how most people see their occupation?

> **ASK:** How can this negative view hinder what God wants to do through our work?

> **ASK:** In what ways has God used your work situation to develop your character and skills, even through a job you don't enjoy?

#4 READ ALOUD: What is the difference between working to contribute to the organization as opposed to working to get from the organization?

> **ASK:** How can you take a step toward making a contribution in your current work environment?

#5 READ ALOUD: The third way to make the office matter is by living on mission with God. This means being salt and light.

> **ASK:** What are some ways that you can partner with God to show God's love to people at work?

WORSHIP AND PRAYER TIME

PRAYER REQUESTS: Ask for everyone's prayer requests. Encourage everyone to share their requests briefly so you can spend more time praying for your requests than talking about them. Be sure to record them on the Small Group Prayer and Praise Report on pages 140-141 of this study guide. Commit to pray for each other's requests every day of the week. Once all the requests are gathered, move into a group worship time.

GROUP WORSHIP AND PRAYER TIME:

Before you pray for each other, invite the presence of the Lord into your time by playing the worship video for this week (Session 4B). As the worship time concludes, flow into your time of prayer by praying over the prayer requests. Encourage the group to participate by praying for one of the prayer requests that were listed.

DISMISSAL

- Talk about the next group meeting.
- Encourage each other to continue to pray for each other throughout the week.

JOURNALING ACTIVITY

Reflect on how you responded to the self-assessment on page 93. Work through the following questions.

- What do you notice about your responses?

_____

_____

_____

_____

_____

_____

_____

_____

_____

_____

If how you approach each day determines your future, what do you need to change now in order to get to that future?

_____

_____

_____

_____

_____

_____

_____

_____

_____

_____

What small things can you do to create new habits at work?

_____

_____

_____

_____

What kind of help do you need to make a change?

_____

_____

_____

_____

How are you sharpening your skills to prepare you for the future?

_____

_____

_____

_____

What do you sense God is saying to you through this?

_____

_____

_____

_____

_____

_____

_____

_____

PRAYER ACTIVITY

In this activity, you will read the passage slowly four times. Many find it helpful to read it aloud. After the first reading, answer the first question. After the second reading, the second question. After the third reading, the third question, and after the fourth time of reading it, answer the fourth question. The passage for this activity is Matthew 5:13-14 NLT.

Question #1: What stands out to you? Don't think about this; just jot down what you see.

_____

_____

_____

_____

_____

_____

_____

Question #2: Is there anything that stirs your heart as you read the passage a second time? If so, write it down.

_____

_____

_____

_____

_____

_____

_____

Question #3: How can you express what you see in this passage into a prayer? Do that now.

_____

_____

_____

_____

_____

_____

_____

_____

Question #4: What do you sense God is saying to you?

_____

_____

_____

_____

_____

_____

_____

_____

_____

_____

_____

_____

_____

_____

RELATIONSHIP ACTIVITY

Make a list in the space below of five or six people with whom you work. Besides their name, identify one way you can pray for them and then ask the Lord to show you one way you can bless them.

NAME	PRAYER	BLESSING

YOU ARE
THE LIGHT
OF THE
WORLD

- Matthew 5:13-14

WEEK 5/DAY 1

Jeremiah 29:5-13 NLT

Our work gets the largest single block of our lives, yet we tend to look for destiny and purpose anywhere but on the job.

In Jeremiah 29, God is speaking to the children of Israel who have been exiled from their Promised Land and into the bondage of foreign Babylon. Jeremiah 29:7 says, "And work for the peace and prosperity of the city where I sent you into exile. Pray to the Lord for it, for its welfare will determine your welfare." God exhorts them not to passively wait for Him to deliver them back to their Promised Land. Rather, He wanted them to be faithful with the work before them.

The children of Israel didn't want to live their lives in Babylon and they probably weren't excited to perform the tasks and duties that were assigned to them either, yet God wanted them to take a higher road. God wanted them to see how their individual labor was connected to the global economy around them. He didn't want them to develop cynical attitudes and lazy habits because of their adversity. He wanted them to overcome by redeeming the world around them through their work.

Now let's read what He says next: "...I will come and do for you all the good things I have promised, and I will bring you home again. For I know the plans I have for you,' says the Lord. 'They are plans for good and not for disaster, to give you a future and a hope'" (verses 10-11). Notice the connection between how they handled their work in the present (Jeremiah 29:5) and the promises God had for them in their future.

When I was young, the Spirit spoke to me personally and powerfully. He said to me,

"If you're faithful with the work in your present, I will be faithful with your future."

I can testify that He has always been faithful to me and can be faithful to you according this pattern found in Jeremiah 29:5-11.

Lord, my future is in Your hands. Because of that, I can be faithful where You currently have me. Thank You that Your grace empowers me to choose You in today's work.

NOTES

WEEK 5/DAY 2

Colossians 3:23-25 NLT

As we live out our God-given design and purpose, "work" is involved. Webster's dictionary defines "work" as:

· To perform or fulfill duties regularly for wages or salary
· To perform or carry through a task requiring sustained effort or continuous repeated operations
· To produce a desired effect or result
· To exert an influence or tendency

According to this definition, even those who are not currently employed find themselves doing "work" of some kind. We are all performing duties, checking off a task list or producing some type of desired result. We have "work" in our careers and we have "work" in our homes.
God's Word encourages us to work willingly and to work for the Lord.

What does this mean? First, it means that we must have sincere and willing hearts, not reluctant but choosing to be favorably disposed toward the tasks at hand.

We choose to be joyful!

We attend meetings with joy; we build houses with joy; we teach with joy; we wash dishes with joy; we mow the lawn with joy; we do homework with joy... you get the picture.

Second, we view our boss as our secondary boss, knowing that our true boss is the Lord. We are not working to make our boss happy - well, okay, we are - however, ultimately, our goal is to please the Lord. The phrase found in these verses is "working for the Lord." This is an interesting concept. It is not that the Lord needs something from us. He desires that we are engaged in meaningful activity that brings glory and honor to His name. When we compete on a team, often the coach will say, "Let's do it for the win!" The coach is implying that the players are to work together giving their very best so that the end result is winning, gaining the prize. We play to win. This same principle can be applied to our work. We work to win. What are we winning? Verse 24 says, "Remember that the Lord will give you an inheritance as your reward."

As we work diligently here on earth with a right heart and joyful attitude, we wait for the reward that is coming: the blessed hope, the joy of knowing we will be with the Lord forever.

PRAYER: Lord, thank You for giving me the capacity to work for You. Give me the ability to view the tasks at hand with joy and a willing heart. Even when the task is something I would rather not do, please help me to see joy in the journey. Thank You for giving me a reward to look forward to. Someday, I will be with You forever. That is a wonderful promise to hold on to and I praise You for Your precious love for me.

NOTES

_____

_____

_____

_____

_____

_____

_____

_____

_____

_____

_____

_____

_____

_____

WEEK 5/DAY 3

Psalm 90:16-17 NLT

In the very beginning of the Bible we see God working, and then resting. There is a trap that some people fall into. They think that God worked in the beginning and then quit working for good. I, for one, am grateful that God kept working and caring for His creation. We can see Him at work throughout the scriptures. We can also see Him at work in our lives.

Ephesians 2:10 tells us that we are God's masterpiece, His signature work. What I love about this is that God created us with purpose. He renewed that purpose through Jesus, and He continues to work in us. All of God's work is good. That is why when I read Psalm 90:16, I joyfully and resoundingly agree, "Yes! God, let me see You work again!" I want to encourage you that as you go through your day and face whatever comes your way, pray, "God, let me see you work in this _____ today."

Another thing to hold onto tightly today is that God is also in our work. Colossians 3:17 says:

> *"And whatever you do or say, do it as a representative of the Lord Jesus, giving thanks through him to God the Father."*

As you enter into your endeavors today, I want to encourage you to remember to work as if you are doing it for God. As you do this, I am confident that Psalm 90:17 will play out true. God will partner with you in your work and help you to be successful.

PRAYER: Lord, You are good. Help me to see where You are working today so that I can partner with You in it. I invite You into my work today. Help me to have joy in my labor, as I am laboring for You!

NOTES

WEEK 5/DAY 4

Proverbs 12:11-12 NLT

As a millennial, I was always told that I could be anything I wanted to be. If I just believed in myself, I could do anything I set my mind to. As I look around at my childhood friends who wanted to be astronauts, pop stars and the President, it's interesting to note that none of us have made it there. It's almost as though we were taught that thoughts and dreams and believing in our own fallible selves would be enough!

Proverbs 12:11 in the NIRV says, "Those who farm their land will have plenty of food. But those who chase dreams have no sense." When we farm the land, we plant seeds that will grow a bountiful harvest. When we put in the work, we will see the reward. It is true of our life's work, in parenting, in relationships and in our worship.

Chasing a dream does nothing but leave you empty-handed and out of breath.

You must capture the dream and let it inspire you to create the plan, construct the frame and build the structure to attain the dream. If you put in the hard work, you will reap the harvest.

What is a dream that the Lord has given you? Sometimes, those dreams seem unreachable. The good news is that if He has called you to it, He will give you the strength and tools necessary to make it there, one step at a time.

Don't resign yourself to a lifetime of just chasing dreams or even forgetting that they're there. Take the God-sized dream and use His direction to guide you in planting the seeds, watering the soil and reaping the harvest that He has for you.

PRAYER: Lord, what is the dream that You want me to work on at this point in my life? I commit to listening for Your voice and doing the work that comes with reaching this dream. Give me the strength and the guidance to do it Your way, and let my life be a testimony of Your faithfulness as I listen and obey.

NOTES

WEEK 5/DAY 5

Proverbs 6:6-11 NLT

As we continue this journey to learn about how our work reflects the glory of God in the form of worship, let's take an in-depth look at Proverbs 6:6-11. Written from the perspective of a parent to a child, the author imparts wisdom and guidance to the reader that is timelessly relevant to our day and age.

When we read this portion of Scripture, the author uses the ant as an illustration to teach us about our work.

It is easy to forget the true value of the occupational tasks we accomplish.

After all, working the day-to-day can become repetitive, easily giving the opportunity to become lazy. However, the author's main point of the expression is that work and how we do it matters, and we must wake up!

God uses our work as a means of tangible provision and can also use our work as a means of evangelism to those around us. When we labor with integrity, with honor and with compassion, we can become an example to all who see of divinely inspired work ethic. Like the ant, it is important for us to wake up and work the way God intended. If we work with no one telling us to do so, doing what we know is right in the sight of the Lord, He provides a blessing for us now, preparing provision for us in the future and using our testimony to be a light in a dark place.

PRAYER: Lord, thank You for Your Word that brings truth and revelation to my life. Show me how to reflect all You are through my work. Continue to mold me as a person of integrity, honor and compassion so my testimony of Your goodness is seen by coworkers, superiors and subordinates.

NOTES

SESSION 6:
NEIGHBORHOOD MATTERS

SCRIPTURE MEMORY:

"But you will receive power when the Holy Spirit comes upon you. And you will be my witnesses, telling people about me everywhere— in Jerusalem, throughout Judea, in Samaria, and to the ends of the earth."

– Acts 1:8, NLT

WELCOME

Give one another five to ten minutes to arrive and get settled in. If possible, provide light snacks and have upbeat music playing in the background.

CHECKING IN

ASK: What is one thing from this series that has impacted you?

PLAY SESSION 6A OF THIS MATTERS VIDEO SERIES AND WRITE DOWN ANYTHING THAT STANDS OUT TO YOU FROM THE TEACHING.

GROUP DISCUSSION QUESTIONS

#1 READ ALOUD: In our world, we tend to focus on ourselves, to be inward focused as we learned in the video teaching.

ASK: How can this mentality hinder how God uses us in the lives of those near us?

#2 ASK A COUPLE OF PEOPLE TO TAKE TURNS READING THE FOLLOWING: LUKE 10:25-37 NLT.

ASK: What stands out to you from this passage?

READ ALOUD: Pastor Nate talked about how we don't get to choose our neighbor. What is Jesus teaching us about what it means to be a neighbor?

#3 READ ALOUD: Use the tic-tac-toe diagram below to identify your neighbors. Put your name in the middle and then write the names of the people who surround you.

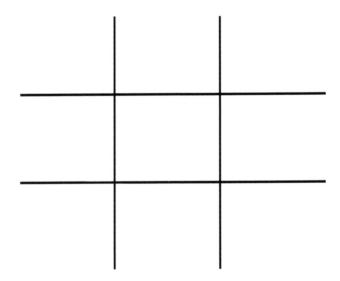

Get into groups of three and pray for the people you have identified for about five minutes.

#4 READ ALOUD: Pastor Nate talked about the importance of depending upon the Holy Spirit when we minister to our neighbors.

> **ASK:** What does it mean for us to depend on the Holy Spirit in this way?

> **ASK:** What is the Holy Spirit saying to you now about your neighbors?

#5 READ ALOUD: Even though this is the final session of this series, it is safe to say that God wants to extend the point of this series beyond these six weeks. We don't have to do huge things, but we can do something that will make an impact.

> **ASK:** What are some ways we can serve our community as a group? We can come up with our own ideas or we can explore some of the ideas on page 123.

WORSHIP AND PRAYER TIME

PRAYER REQUESTS: Ask for everyone's prayer requests. Encourage everyone to share their requests briefly so you can spend more time praying for your requests than talking about them. Be sure to record them on the Small Group Prayer and Praise Report on pages 140-141 of this study guide. Commit to pray for each other's requests every day of the week. Once all the requests are gathered, move into a group worship time.

GROUP WORSHIP AND PRAYER TIME:

 Before you pray for each other, invite the presence of the Lord into your time by playing the worship video for this week (Session 6B). As the worship time concludes, flow into your time of prayer by praying over the prayer requests. Encourage the group to participate by praying for one of the prayer requests that were listed.

DISMISSAL

- Talk about the next group meeting.
- Encourage each other to continue to pray for each other throughout the week.

JOURNALING ACTIVITY

Reflect on the names of the people whose names you wrote in the tic-tac-toe diagram on page 115. (If you don't know the names of some of your neighbors, make an effort to meet them.)

_____

_____

_____

_____

_____

In the following tic-tac-toe diagram, write out the names of your neighbors again but list any needs they might have as well. Spend some time praying for each person by name.

_____

_____

_____

_____

_____

_____

_____

_____

_____

_____

_____

_____

_____

Write down any impressions that you sense as you pray. Ask the Lord to create opportunities to connect with your neighbors, to open doors for deeper interactions. Make sure you write down what occurs.

PRAYER ACTIVITY

In this activity, you will read the passage slowly four times. Many find it helpful to read it aloud. After the first reading, answer the first question. After the second reading, the second question. After the third reading, the third question, and after the fourth time of reading it, answer the fourth question. The passage for this activity is Acts 1:8 NLT.

Question #1: What stands out to you? Don't think about this; just jot down what you see.

_____

_____

_____

_____

_____

_____

_____

Question #2: Is there anything that stirs your heart as you read the passage a second time? If so, write it down.

_____

_____

_____

_____

_____

_____

_____

Question #3: How can you express what you see in this passage into a prayer? Do that now.

_____

_____

_____

_____

_____

_____

_____

_____

Question #4: What do you sense God is saying to you?

_____

_____

_____

_____

_____

_____

_____

_____

_____

_____

_____

_____

_____

_____

RELATIONSHIP ACTIVITY

Review the list below of ways that you might visibly act to make a difference in your local context (community, schools, neighborhood, etc). Pray over it. See what grabs you. Then meet with a friend and/ or a small group to discuss what you are feeling compelled to do. See if another person feels a similar compulsion or if someone might join you. Then make a plan to do it. After you do it, sit down with your friend or your small group and talk about how it went. Here are some questions to guide the conversation:

- What did you enjoy?
- What was the most challenging?
- How did you sense God moving?
- What would you do differently?
- What's next?

_____

_____

_____

Ideas for ministering to your neighbors:
- Throw a party at your house or in a neighborhood clubhouse and invite your neighbors.
- Host a coffee and dessert night.
- Lead a food drive or coat drive and ask the neighbors if they want to participate.
- Participate in homeowners' association meetings.
- Start an exercise group in the neighborhood.
- Lead a book group and invite neighbors to suggest books they might want to read.
- Throw a block party.
- Use a unique skill or gift to bless others. For instance, if you like working on cars, have an oil change day. If you enjoy baking, host a cooking class. Mow the yard or weed the garden of a neighbor.
- Purchase some extra groceries and drop them by the home of a neighbor who needs some extra food.
- Borrow a tool or a cup of sugar from a neighbor. One way to tear down walls in a relationship is to allow others to bless you. It puts them at ease.

BUT YOU WILL RECEIVE POWER WHEN THE HOLY SPIRIT COMES UPON YOU

- Acts 1:8

WEEK 6/DAY 1

Mark 12:29-31 NLT

Often it can be so easy to be caught up in our own agenda that we forget to see the needs of others around us! But look around! How many people are lonely and isolated? God created us to be in relationship with one another and while it is unrealistic to be there for everyone all the time, we still are told to love those around us and love them well. Caring for those around us doesn't need to be complicated. In fact, it's pretty simple. It means showing up. It means being there in the highs and in the lows. Of course, it also sometimes requires us to put our needs aside and put others first.

We all have people that we connect to, but God didn't tell us to just love people who are super easy to love and who had everything in common with us.

Has God highlighted someone to you that you should be connecting with? Maybe it's a coworker or boss that you could go out to coffee with and get to know better. Maybe it's your cousin who you don't see very often but you feel the need to call and check in on. God calls us to love Him and then love others.

This week, let's pray about who God might be wanting us to reach out to and then reach out to them! Let's be people who love on those around us and are known for being full of love! (I know it might sound cheesy and fluttery, but for real, what's life without some love?)

PRAYER: Lord, help me to see those around me who are in need. Please show me how to show those around me the love that You have for them! You are such a loving God and for that, I am so thankful.

NOTES

WEEK 6/DAY 2

Luke 10:30-37 NLT

Jesus tells this story in reply to a very simple, but complex question: "Who is my neighbor?"
How we choose to respond to the needs around us ultimately determines who our neighbor is.

Jesus told this story to strongly challenge a way of thinking that was more focused on self than on seeing others. I know I can come up with a list of reasons why I can't help when there's a need. ...I'm too busy, I can't afford to, someone else can do it....

There are people in our path all the time. Sometimes the needs are huge and other times they are small and seemingly insignificant. Either way, we can find it easy to see past the need rather than see into the need.

We are busy and preoccupied people, so oftentimes, we look the other way, we pass by or we ignore what we see. But once we have seen a need, we now have a responsibility to determine what we can and should do about it.

> *This world doesn't care what our religion looks like on Sunday morning. This world cares if we are willing to show mercy to someone in their time of need.*

Being a neighbor is not about proximity. Being a neighbor is about taking the time to care.
We don't get to pick and choose who God brings across our path, but we do get to choose how we will respond. Will we pass by or will we take the time to show kindness and care to someone in need?

I want to encourage you today. You don't need to have all of the answers or know exactly what you're supposed to do to solve the problem. Once you see a need, showing mercy simply begins as it did for the good Samaritan: by walking to the person and doing what he could to show care.

PRAYER: *Lord, give me eyes to see the needs of people around me that You have brought across my path. Give me a heart of compassion and the capacity to show care and mercy. Thank you that when I was in my time of need, You showed mercy and compassion to me.*

NOTES

WEEK 6/DAY 3

Matthew 5:13-16 NLT

I read this scripture and I read it as a call and commission for every believer in Jesus Christ. It's a giving of purpose to share this beautiful news and amazing relationship with Jesus we have been given.

When we live as the preservers of the Gospel here on earth and the carriers of the light of Christ to the world, the world gets the opportunity to know Him and He gets the glory. When we talk about the world, it is often in reference to "the big picture" world or "grand scheme" culture, but let's narrow the scope a little. It is also the people you rub shoulders with everyday.

Whether you live in the heart of Minneapolis or in the suburbs of Maple Grove or anywhere in between, why not start with these people who live closest to us? Maybe it looks like bringing a meal to the family of six next door or starting a conversation with the homeless girl on the corner down the block from your apartment or being thankful to the person scanning your items at the store or even showing grace and patience to the worker who got your order wrong at your local Chick-Fil-A. Whatever it is, we cannot live this halfway.

Salt cannot be halfway salty, and light cannot be halfway lit.

This isn't about living in the security of a church building or social standing, but in the security that God Himself is with us and living inside us and calling us to be His church. Let's start today with those who live closest to us! This is a faith journey, so take a step of faith today, knowing that the One who gave you this call is also the One who will see it through to the end.

PRAYER: Lord, as I go about my day, remind me that I can bring Your light to the people I interact with on a daily basis. Show me what to say and how to say it; may my actions glorify You and shine light on Your kingdom.

NOTES

_____

_____

_____

_____

_____

_____

_____

_____

_____

_____

_____

_____

_____

_____

_____

_____

_____

_____

_____

_____

_____

_____

_____

WEEK 6/DAY 4

Colossians 4:2-5 NLT

Prayer is one of the most powerful and important things we could do as human beings.

Prayer gains us access to God and all of His greatness!

Wow! I stay amazed at just that simple thought about prayer. We have access to Him! But do all the people around us have access to Him? The answer is yes! They can have access to God, but how will they know? It's God's mission for us to share the love of Jesus Christ to all and to care for our neighbors, and the way we need to do that is by building relationships with them. The invitation of opportunity comes by building intentional relationships.

I'm a strong believer that opportunity comes through the network that is built upon relationship. Our role as Christ-followers is to be the "salt and light of the world" (Matthew 5:13-16). God wants us to be reflections of His light in a dark world. He wants us to be representatives of His great love for all people and sharers of the eternal hope we have in Jesus. Our world needs Jesus and we as Christ-followers are called to tell others about Him.

How do we do that? By living in a way that reflects Jesus in every way. By praying for our neighbors. By being a positive person around others. By showing love to everyone, regardless of their background, race, religion, political views, gender, etc. By simply being a good neighbor that will make the most of every relational encounter.

Verse 5 tells us to "make the most of every opportunity." Let's make every moment count for the sake of the Gospel of Jesus Christ. Let's not just talk to others about Jesus; let's show them Jesus!

PRAYER: Lord, help me be intentional with every moment and every person. Even in the hard times, may I aim to reflect Your love to the people around me.

NOTES

WEEK 6/DAY 5

Acts 1:4-8 NLT

The first chapter in the book of Acts paints an exciting scene in the story of God's people. The risen Christ appears to the disciples and reminds them of the mission He's entrusting them. After passing off the baton of proclaiming hope and Good News, He ascends into heaven.

The disciples probably weren't even aware how pivotal that moment was. In fact, they were a bit oblivious to what God was doing. They asked Jesus about their own kingdom, losing sight of the fact that He was ushering in a kingdom not of this world. They were concerned with timing and missed seeing the big picture of God's overarching plan for the world.

Jesus gently redirects their attention to what really matters. "It's not for you to know the when.
And it's really not about your own kingdom. Remember what really matters and get involved in what God is doing today to impact the world. Start from where you are at and be a firsthand witness of God's hope for the world."

I wonder how often we get caught up in the wrong questions or tangled up with the wrong concerns.

The truth is it's not about our kingdom, our plans or our expectations. It's about God's values and what truly matters to Him. We're reminded in this portion of Acts as with the whole of Scripture narrative that there is a value central to God's heart: people. Humanity has moved God to sacrifice His Son for salvation and hope. Humanity is the reason He mobilizes His church to spread His Good News.

People have always mattered to God. Because they matter to Him, they should matter to us. Let's join our hearts with God and align our efforts with His!

PRAYER: Lord, give me clarity on what truly matters in life. Help me understand what moves Your heart and move my heart in the same direction. Guide me to take steps that reflect Your compassion and the hope that You've ignited within me. Teach me to love people the way You do.

NOTES

CONCLUSION

We hope you've enjoyed the experience of THIS MATTERS! Our prayer is that what matters the most in your life will rise above the distraction and noise of this age. We also pray that your group setting will become a circle of continual encouragement and growth in your life.

Our aim and heart is that you will be empowered to live with purpose each day of your life.

SMALL GROUP RESOURCES

Small Group Guidelines

Small Group Roster

Prayer & Praise Report

SMALL GROUP GUIDELINES

It's a good idea for everyone to put words to their shared values, expectations and commitments. Such guidelines will help avoid unspoken agendas and unmet expectations. We recommend you discuss your guidelines during Session One to lay the foundation for a healthy group experience. Feel free to modify anything that doesn't work for your group.

WE AGREE TO THESE VALUES:

CLEAR PURPOSE	To grow healthy spiritual lives by building a healthy small group community.
GROUP ATTENDANCE	To give priority to the group meeting (call if absent or late)
SAFE ENVIRONMENT	To create a safe place where people can be heard and feel loved (no quick answers, snap judgments or simple fixes)
BE CONFIDENTIAL	To keep anything that is shared strictly confidential within the group
CONFLICT RESOLUTION	To avoid gossip and immediately resolve concerns by following the principles of Matthew 18:15-17
SPIRITUAL HEALTH	To give group members permission to speak into my life and help me live a healthy, balanced spiritual life
LIMIT OUR FREEDOM	To limit our freedom by not serving or consuming alcohol during group activities so as to avoid causing a weaker member to stumble (1 Cor. 8:1-13; Romans 14:19-21)

WELCOME NEWCOMERS	To invite friends who might benefit from this study and warmly welcome newcomers
SCRIPTURE	While everyone's thoughts and opinions are valuable and encouraged, to ultimately rely on the truth of Scripture as our final authority
BUILDING RELATIONSHIPS	To get to know the other members of the group and pray for them regularly

SMALL GROUP ROSTER

NAME	PHONE	EMAIL

PRAYER & PRAISE REPORT

This is a place where you can write each other's requests for prayer. You can also make a note when God answers a prayer. Pray for each other's requests. If you're new to group prayer, it's okay to pray silently or to pray by using just one sentence:

"God, please help _____ to _____."

DATE	PERSON	PRAYER REQUEST	PRAISE

PRAYER & PRAISE REPORT (cont'd)

DATE	PERSON	PRAYER REQUEST	PRAISE

Made in the USA
San Bernardino, CA
26 July 2020